SEQUOIA
&
KINGS CANYON
NATIONAL PARKS

A PLACE WHERE
GIANTS DWELL
BY
GEORGE B. ROBINSON

SIERRA PRESS
MARIPOSA, CA

DEDICATION

Harry B. Robinson, my father, mentor, and hero almost reached his goal of living 100 years, many of which he enjoyed working in America's National Parks. He counted among his most memorable experiences the time he spent in Sequoia and Kings Canyon. I miss you Dad. This book is for you.

—G.B.R.

ACKNOWLEDGMENTS

I am grateful to Jeff Nicholas, at Sierra Press, for his continued faith in my writing, and to my editor Nicky Leach for her honest, thoughtful, and encouraging critique of my work. I owe special thanks to William C. Tweed, Chief of Interpretation in Sequoia and Kings Canyon National Parks. During a busy time, Bill graciously reviewed the manuscript for accuracy. Each of these people made my words sound better.   —G.B.R.

INSIDE FRONT COVER
Giant sequoias in Giant Forest.
PHOTO ©LARRY ULRICH
TITLE PAGE
The General Sherman Tree, winter in Giant Forest.
PHOTO ©RONALD G. WARFIELD
PAGE 4 (BELOW)
Tokopah Falls, Lodgepole area.
PHOTO ©DENNIS FLAHERTY
PAGE 4/5
Dusy Basin, summer sunset.
PHOTO ©LARRY CARVER
PAGE 6/7
Shooting stars in Crescent Meadow, Giant Forest.
PHOTO ©FRED HIRSCHMANN
PAGE 7 (LOWER RIGHT)
Late afternoon view from near Moro Rock.
PHOTO ©TOM ALGIRE

4

CONTENTS

THE SETTING 9
  THE LOCATION 11
  THE PARKS 12
  THE GEOLOGIC STORY 14/15
  HUMAN HISTORY 16/17

THE FOOTHILLS 19
  ELEVATION, CLIMATE, AND LIFE 21
  THE UNDERWORLD 22

THE FOREST 25
  GIANT FOREST 27
  GRANT GROVE 30
  FRIENDLY FIRE 33
  SOMETHING IN THE AIR 34

THE CANYON COUNTRY 39
  KINGS CANYON/CEDAR GROVE 41
  THE RIVERS 42

THE HIGH COUNTRY 45
  MINERAL KING 47
  MANAGEMENT MILESTONES 48

THE WILD THINGS 51
  A GUIDE TO THE ANIMALS 55
  A GUIDE TO THE PLANTS 56
  A WORD ABOUT BEARS 58

RESOURCES & INFORMATION 62/63

THE SETTING

Wild strawberry, Redwood Mountain Grove.   PHOTO ©RANDI HIRSCHMANN

This is the forest primeval.
The murmuring pines and the hemlocks,
Bearded with moss, and in garments green, indistinct in the twilight,
Stand like Druids of eld.
Henry Wadsworth Longfellow

On Specimen Ridge in Yellowstone National Park, jutting up from 40-million-year-old volcanic debris, there is a petrified stump more than 26 feet around. It is a fossilized sequoia. Big Trees once flourished here and in other ancient landscapes, but now they only survive in the distant Sierra Nevada, where they are best appreciated in Sequoia and King Canyon National Parks.

I first entered Sequoia and Kings Canyon National Parks more than forty years ago—only a moment in the lifetime of a sequoia tree. Some of the ancient trees that I walked among then still had a thousand years to live. I am much older now but the venerable sequoias show few signs of aging, other than adding several cubic feet of new growth each year. The trees rise from the forest floor—as they have for centuries—like massive living colonnades of layered tissue sheathed in deeply furrowed bark. I long to see them again, so I travel to the parks on a memory trip.

Walking among the sequoias, I feel like a dwarf in the presence of antiquated monarchs. They prompt me to consider the brevity of human life and the folly of believing that people have dominion over wild things. How can I question the sovereignty of nature when I'm standing in a gallery of some of her finest works? Nature's mastery of form, function, endurance, and beauty is evident in every fluted cinnamon trunk and bushy crown.

Edward Abbey said, "The purpose of the giant sequoia tree is to provide shade for the tiny titmouse." His words remind me that small things too are part of nature's plan. This place where giants dwell would be incomplete without the slime mold and the newt. Stone is crumbled piecemeal by a living veneer of lichen. A few drops of water trapped in a rocky fissure have the latent sculpting power of glacial ice. However large organisms may grow, all spring from a single cell.

Sequoias are emblematic of these parks. They dominate the woods in bulk and appearance yet, looking beyond the forest, I see older and larger things. Each is a player, prop, or setting in the continuing drama of nature.

The stage is the Sierra Nevada. It is a mountain range composed mostly of granite, an igneous rock. The ancestral mountains were created by the collision of two huge pieces of the earth's crust, which drift about on molten rock beneath the surface. The collision forced the ocean floor down under the continent's western margin, giving birth to a range rising nearly three miles above the sea. The mountains were then exposed to the cosmetic effects of wind, rain, snow, and ice, which sculpted the rough-hewn rock into the smoother surfaces I see today.

According to the protocols of nature, what goes up must eventually come down. Thus, the forces of erosion and weathering chafe and peel the skin of the mountains and carry it into the foothills and valleys below. These loose mountain sediments accumulate in the lowlands. With time, they harden once more into rocks, and eventually rise again to repeat the cycle.

The Sierra is a vertical world—a place of tall mountains and deep canyons. It rises from about 500 feet above sea level in the foothills abutting the San Joaquin Valley to more than 14,000 feet along the backbone of the range.

As if to counter the elevating effect of the mountains, moving water and ice have cut into hard bedrock, indelibly marking it with deep canyons. The first incisions by streams and rivers were steep-walled and angular. Later, ice-age glaciers, burdened with abrasives scraped away by ice as it moved, flowed down the pathways created by early watercourses. The rasplike effect of ice broadened and deepened the canyons, softening their contours. Many of the canyons in Sequoia country are several thousand feet deep.

Geological processes have fashioned a landscape hospitable to life. The Big Trees are just the largest living things here. Because of the changes in elevation—more than 500 feet with each mile—conditions range from hot, arid foothills up through dense, moist forests to barren alpine boulder fields and peaks chilled by per-

Evening light on Mount Huxley, Evolution Basin.

petual wind. A great diversity of habitats and ecological niches exist, and they are filled with all sorts of plants and animals. These living communities change depending on their tolerance of different conditions at each elevation. It's as if they live on different floors of the same high-rise building.

Chamise, blue oak, and yucca thrive in the dry lowlands while incense cedar, sequoia, red fir, and foxtail pine enjoy increasingly higher elevations. Ithuriel's spear and baby blue eyes add color to the lower slopes while sky pilots and shooting stars adorn the high fells. Striped skunks, scorpions, and California quail prefer warmer, drier climes, yet they live only a few miles from the home of black bears, pine martens, and porcupines. Still higher, marmots sun themselves on glacially polished rocks while pikas busily harvest grass for their miniature haystacks.

I am not alone in this place. Wild eyes follow me wherever I wander. Mountains, valleys, and forests embrace and nurture me. I see written in the rocks and the ways of wild things the wisdom and artistry of nature, and I feel that I have come home.

Mule deer in Zumwalt Meadow.

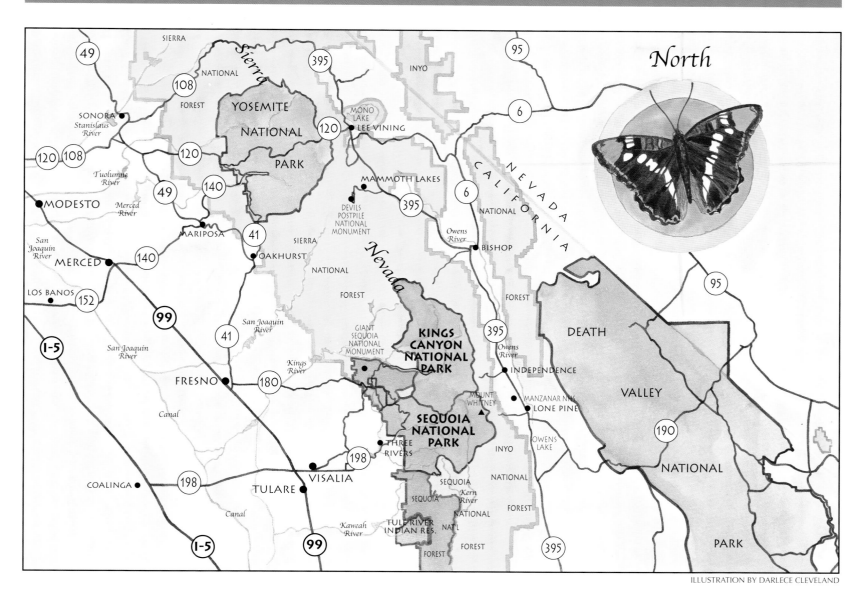

ILLUSTRATION BY DARLECE CLEVELAND

Sequoia and Kings Canyon National Parks include a total of 864,383 acres of the southern Sierra Nevada—the highest part of the range. On a map they look like two conjoined pieces of a jigsaw puzzle.

Actually, the comparison is quite accurate. During the last few decades, our perceptions of national parks have changed. Although parks are popularly believed to be secure islands, insulated from external influence, there has been a growing awareness that parks exist in a much larger ecological context—that they are parts of much larger systems.

In nature, boundaries are often indistinct; they are drawn by the resources and ecological processes that link them, not by the territorial imperatives of people. All ecosystems, from a miniature community of lichens growing on a few square inches of granite to an area that includes the entire Sierra Nevada, have edges. But, their edges are not hard, straight, and angular. Rather, like living things, they are soft, pliable, constantly changing. In the world of people, boundaries denote ownership, a concept that has no meaning in nature—although many animals fiercely defend their territories.

The wisdom of considering a Sequoia and Kings Canyon unbound by political lines is confirmed by our knowledge that living organisms don't see or respect boundaries that people have drawn on a map. Neither do the natural processes that connect them. With the concept of a much larger ecosystem in mind, it is easier to understand how activities beyond the boundary of the parks can profoundly affect the resources within. For example, airborne pollutants from lowland cities have caused declines in amphibian populations and resulted in the defoliation of many ponderosa and Jeffrey pines.

Park ecosystems are aggregations of countless smaller systems. Each is discrete and essentially self-sustaining, yet all are connected through the perpetual motion of ecological process. The greater ecosystem represents the whole organism, not just the heart. It is the larger context of life and environment in which each smaller system operates, and upon which they rely for their health and vitality.

Acknowledging these fundamental truths, scientists and resource managers look beyond conventional legal boundaries for relationships and connections. Our field of vision has been broadened to include what are called greater ecosystems— a description that aptly conveys a sense that parks are just pieces of a much larger puzzle.

Sequoia and Kings Canyon National Parks include 864,383 acres of pristine Sierra Nevada landscape—some of the finest parts of a range in which uncommon beauty is a common quality. All of the classic elements of national parks are here: spectacular mountains; forests; crystal-clear rivers and lakes; miles of caves; waterfalls; deep, river-cut canyons; glacially scoured valleys; thousands of plants; and unfettered wild animals.

Although they were created by separate acts of Congress, they share a common boundary and are managed as one park. Sequoia was established in 1890—18 years after Yellowstone. It is America's second national park.

Nearly one and a half million people make pilgrimages to these natural shrines each year, approaching from the west via State Route 99. The Big Stump entrance provides access via State Highway 180 from Fresno to Grant Grove and Cedar Grove, both in Kings Canyon National Park. State Highway 198 passes through Visalia and ends at the boundary of Sequoia National Park near the Ash Mountain entrance. Mineral King and the extreme southern part of Sequoia can be reached on partially paved roads from Highway 198. No roads cross the Sierra into the parks.

At the Big Stump and Ash Mountain entrances, park rangers greet visitors, collect fees, and distribute maps and guides. The road connecting the two entrances is called The Generals Highway. It provides access to the foothills, Giant Forest, Lodgepole, and Grant Grove, where visitor centers or museums are located. At each facility there are information desks, exhibits, audiovisual programs, and bookstores featuring theme-related interpretive materials. Accessible public restrooms are located in each building, and pay phones are available everywhere but the Giant Forest Museum.

Most of the 14 campgrounds in the combined parks are available on a first-come, first-served basis. All campgrounds are operated by the National Park Service, but in two campgrounds reservations may be made through a private company. Modest fees range from $8 to $16. Hotels, restaurants, gift shops, and stores are operated by park concessionaires. It is a good idea to make reservations well in advance of your visit—a year is not too early!

To learn more about Sequoia and Kings Canyon, their geology, plant and animal life, and human history, check out the exhibits at visitor centers, or participate in an interpretive program. The ranger-guided walks, campfire programs, demonstrations, and other activities are available to people of all ages, free of charge—except at Crystal Cave. They are your chance to get to know these two magnificent parks better.

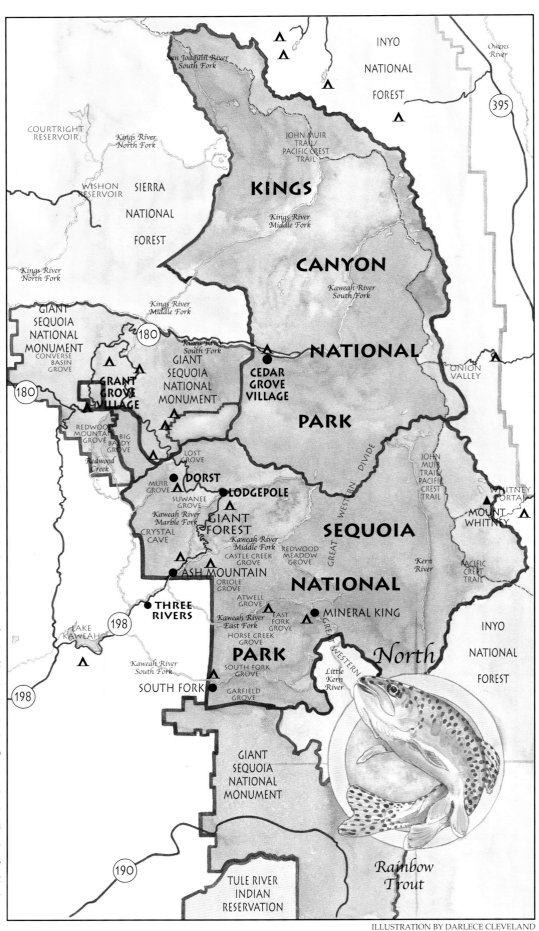

ILLUSTRATION BY DARLECE CLEVELAND

OPPOSITE: Giant sequoias and thimbleberry next to The Generals Highway. PHOTO ©LARRY ULRICH

The earth is 5 billion years old, give or take a few million years. The first millennium of the Christian era has just passed, so I have a vague idea of the length of a thousand years, but how long is a million years? A billion? My father lived almost a hundred years—more than most people can expect. Yet, these mountains that he loved and worked in long ago are geologically young. In order to grasp the scope of geologic time, I need to look at a different sort of clock.

Back in the 1950s, James C. Rettie wrote a scientific fable called *But a Watch in the Night,* in which he tried to make geologic time more understandable by relating it to an imaginary time-lapse motion picture of the earth filmed at one frame each year. The completed movie, run at the normal speed of 24 frames per second, would depict 24 years of earth history every second; 1,440 years per minute; 86,400 years per hour; approximately 2 million years per day; and 62 million years per month. If it were projected at your local theater and continued running for one year beginning at midnight on New Year's Eve, by the following New Year's Eve, you still would only have seen about one-sixth of the earth's history, or the last 757 million years. In this amazing fictitious movie, a human lifespan occupies about three seconds, and the Sierra doesn't appear until near the end of the film.

Change is an enduring aspect of the process that we call nature, but in the short span of my life any alterations to the landscape are often barely perceptible. The changes I have experienced occurred as a result of sudden, sometimes spectacular events. An avalanche toppling hundred-year-old trees. A flash flood gouging a new stream channel. An earthquake triggering a rock fall that reshapes a mountainside.

Most often, slow and endless geological processes create a kind of stone "book" whose pages are made up of rock formations that record mountain time in millions of years. As wind scours the rock and rivers of water and ice move

relentlessly over it, they prise open the pages of the stony book, revealing evidence of the geologic past. The peaks and valleys of the Sierra are a geological masterpiece. Wondering about their origin I recall the words of scientist James F. Trefil. In his book *Meditations at 10,000 Feet*, he writes, "the appearance of a rock, like the appearance of a person, tells you something about the sort of life it has had."

Geologists have read the story in the rocks and pieced together a picture of how the Sierra

Nevada were formed. About 500 million years ago, the region where the Sierra Nevada now stands lay beneath the sea, where tens of thousands of feet of sediments from the continent accumulated and eventually formed limestone, sandstone, and other sedimentary rocks, which extended the shoreline to the west.

The Sierra sit on a giant piece of land called a continental, or tectonic, plate. The North American Plate is actually a huge section of the earth's brittle crust, which drifts about on the mantle, a sea of partially melted rock that encircles the inner layers of the globe. It is a remnant of a huge primordial land mass called Pangaea, which split up some 300 million years ago, setting its disembodied parts adrift like giant puzzle pieces. Convection currents in the plastic mantle, heated by intense pressure and radioactive decay, cause movement of the plates.

Approximately 100 million years ago, the North American Plate drifted to the southwest and collided with the Pacific Plate, which was moving eastward. The continental plate rode up over the edge of the oceanic plate, forcing it down under the continental margin in a process called subduction.

The pressure and friction of the plates moving past each other caused the crust of the Pacific Plate to melt, forming plumes of molten rock that began to extend up through the underside of the continent. These plutons, as geologists call them, merged and cooled to form a single, massive deeply imbedded rock structure called a batholith. It formed the heart of the future Sierra Nevada.

The batholith began to rise during a mountain building episode (an orogeny) about 80

ABOVE: Glacially-polished granite above the Kaweah River drainage. PHOTO ©CARR CLIFTON

million years ago. The embryonic mountains pushed up under earlier marine sediments, which were then eroded and carried back down to the lowlands. Remnants of the marine rock, called roof pendants, still cling to some mountain tops. The uplift was caused by the vertical movement of massive blocks of rock, relative to one another, along splits, or faults, in the earth. Movement was greatest on the eastern side of the batholith, so the Sierra Nevada tilts toward the west, creating a gradual western slope and a precipitous incline on the eastern side. The uplift continued—most of it occurring during the last 10 million years—creating mountains that were several thousand feet higher than those of the Sierra today.

Once the Sierra Nevada was formed, rivers and glaciers reshaped it. Rivers cut deep canyons and carried tons of sediment back down to the lowlands building thousands of feet of rich alluvial soil. As valley floors grew, mountains became correspondingly lower. During the Ice Age, glaciers covered much of the range. Their great weight caused them to slide downhill, where they flowed into the angular canyons that rivers had formed.

As glaciers moved, they plucked pebbles, rocks, and boulders from canyon walls and floors, imbedding them in ice, like diamond particles on a burr. Abrasive-laden ice added to the work of moving water by scraping and polishing the rough-cut rock. The rivers abide, but only traces of the icy sculptors remain on remote slopes, where they are gradually retreating.

Three types of rocks are found here. Sedimentary rocks are formed by the accumulation and hardening of sediments like sand, mud, and lime deposits. Metamorphic rocks are rocks altered underground by pressure, heat, or chemical changes. Igneous rocks—the most prevalent in the Sierra—form when molten rock, or magma, cools and solidifies at depth.

I examine a piece of granite with a hand lens and see that it is composed of a mosaic of inter-

locking particles. In rocks like granite, the particles are sometimes big enough to be seen with the naked eye. These particles are minerals. Minerals are naturally occurring materials that have definite chemical compositions, and physical properties. Minerals are the geologic analogs to the cells that combine to form living organisms. There are hundreds of different types of minerals, each with its distinctive chemical composition and crystalline structure, but some are more common than others.

Granite is a coarse-grained igneous rock containing mainly quartz and feldspar and smaller quantities of mica, hornblende, and other dark minerals. Granite is the main rock of these mountains. It is found along with gneiss, a metamorphic rock with thick, dark-colored streaks, formed when granite comes into contact with superheated molten rock, or magma, deep below the earth's surface. Schist is a fine-grained metamorphic rock that contains many parallel grains of mica (a smooth, shiny, mineral that flakes into thin flexible pieces). Marble is the metamorphic offspring of limestone, while sandstone is changed into quartzite.

Why do I study these rocks? Because they are fundamental to my understanding of the natural history of the parks. Geological processes gave birth to the mountains of the Sierra Nevada, and influenced their maturity. Geological features control the movement of water. The weather, climate, and microclimate are affected by geology. Geology shapes the environment, and the environment controls the development of communities of plants and animals. The geologic structure of the Sierra Nevada is the foundation on which the living systems of the watershed are built.

It occurs to me that—though it appears solid—rock has some of the same properties as the "silly putty" I played with as a child. It can be marked with an edge tool. If it is heated it will flow and conform to a surface. It can be slowly stretched and folded upon itself, yet if it's pulled abruptly apart it can break. So it was when the Sierra was born.

ABOVE: The dramatically glaciated landscape at Arctic Lake, near Mount Whitney. PHOTO ©GEORGE WUERTHNER

HUMAN HISTORY

Toward the end of the Great Ice Age, 10,000 or more years ago, early people ventured into the region from the north. Few in number, they were probably nomadic hunters in search of migratory ice-age game. These early visitors, living on the edge of survival, were the first in a long procession of people drawn to this area. They were harbingers of a time—still thousands of years away—when millions of their descendants would visit the Sierra each year, searching for understanding and enjoyment of nature.

Archeologists have found evidence of several very early cultures that apparently spread south into North America and evolved in response to changing climate, vegetation, and animal life. Those changes are partially inferred from differences in the type of projectile points used by the paleo-hunters. The points suggest, in turn, changes in the nature of what was being hunted. These habitation sites and other artifacts confirm the continued presence of people in this region over several thousand years.

Later groups of more settled Native Americans were the first to venture into the Sierra Nevada. They followed the movements of game animals and were probably seeking refuge from summer heat. Once there, we can imagine them communing with wild icons in their spiritual world and, possibly, just enjoying the untrammeled beauty of the place. Native peoples wintered in large encampments such as Hospital Rock, near Ash Mountain. They harvested acorns from oak trees, and drew water from the Middle Fork of the Kaweah River. These foothill villages were used year-round.

Abundant evidence of these early visitors has been found and includes stone mortars—smooth, shallow depressions in rocks used to grind acorns into flour for bread and porridge. Points and discarded flakes of obsidian, a type of shiny, black volcanic glass, are common. They, and other material evidence, suggest that native people used projectiles to hunt animals in both the foothills and the high country.

It's known that people of the Western Mono, Tubatulabal, Paiute, and Yokut tribal groups visited or lived in this part of the Sierra for many years. Sadly, in the 1860s, Native American populations were nearly wiped out by contagious diseases introduced by white settlers in the San Joaquin Valley a decade earlier.

While a party of Spanish missionaries named the Kings River in January 1806, there is no indication that they actually entered the mountains. It wasn't until the latter part of the 1800s that Euro-Americans entered the Sierra Nevada. A few survey parties may have tentatively edged into the foothills, but the first Euro-American to see the sequoias in Giant Forest was Hale Tharp in the mid–1840s. Ironically, he was more interested in grass than in giant trees.

When he arrived, he found many native villages—villages that he later saw decimated by measles. Local Indians guided him to the Giant Forest in 1858. Tharp was searching for summer range for his cattle. No doubt Tharp was struck by the great size of the trees, but he was more impressed by the lush meadows, which he and family members used to graze cattle for the latter half of the century and early 1900s. Tharp's tangible legacy to Sequoia National Park is the primitive—yet still sound—cabin that he fashioned in the end of a dead sequoia tree at Log Meadow.

Perhaps Tharp's most significant accomplishment is that he introduced naturalist John Muir—a wandering disciple of transcendentalist writer Henry David Thoreau—to Giant Forest in 1873. Unlike Hale Tharp, Muir was on a quest for knowledge and understanding of wild America. Impressed by his first visit to Grant Grove and Kings Canyon, Muir returned in 1875 to explore all the groves to the south. He said that after "…general exploration of the Kaweah Basin, this part of the sequoia belt seemed to me the finest…." He called the grove Giant Forest, and later his lyrical writings and outspoken advocacy would help lead to the establishment of Sequoia National Park.

Prior to Muir's journey of discovery a

ABOVE: Potholes in the foothills near Hospital Rock. PHOTO ©FRED HIRSCHMANN

few trappers and prospectors probably passed through the area, but soon other people—seeking wealth of a different sort—learned of the giant trees, and of possible mineral deposits in the region.

Starting in 1863–1864, during a great drought, Basque sheepherders worked their flocks in the watersheds of the Kern and Kaweah Rivers. In 1873, prospectors—some of whom may have been drawn to California by the 1849 Gold Rush—discovered silver in the Mineral King area. Mines were built, and some ore was extracted. Less than five years after Muir's visit to Giant Forest, a mining company built a road into Mineral King, but the mines soon played out. Both the sheep and the road foreshadowed later problems.

As more and more people flocked to the region in the 1870s, the demand for lumber increased. Lumber companies learned of the giant sequoias and other large trees on the tablelands and began to cut down and mill pine and fir trees as well as several sequoias. Evidence of the fate of those sequoias can be seen today at Big Stump Basin in Kings Canyon National Park. During the logging period a few sequoias, including the Centennial, Mark Twain, and General Noble Trees, as well as cross-sections, were cut and sent back east, where they were displayed to a skeptical public. Surely, they said, no trees could be that large.

In 1885, a short-lived social experiment took place in what would become Sequoia National Park a few years later. A man named Burnette Haskell and a group of followers filed claims to virtually all of the Giant Forest area with the intention of logging the forest to help finance the creation of a utopian society they called the Kaweah Colony. With the creation of Sequoia National Park and the later addition of Giant Forest, the elaborate utopian dream was lost, and the colony soon dissolved.

Near the end of the 19th century, growing local concern over the preservation of

unexploited areas of the southern Sierra Nevada, including the giant sequoias, led to a movement for protective legislation. On September 25, 1890, 18 years after the creation of Yellowstone National Park, Congress authorized the establishment of Sequoia National Park in an act signed into law by President Benjamin Harrison.

A few days later, another law created General Grant National Park and tripled the size of Sequoia. In 1940, General Grant National Park became part of the newly authorized Kings Canyon National Park, established to preserve the unparalleled peaks, canyons, rivers, lakes, and forests north of Sequoia. Mineral King Valley, to the south, remained vulnerable to development until it was added to Sequoia in 1978, bringing the total size of the two parks to 864,383 nearly 1,400 square miles.

The recent decision to remove visitor facilities from overused developed areas in the parks, and to undertake large restoration projects, especially in Giant Forest, is likely to have increasing historical significance as time goes on. The action paves the way for other national parks with overuse problems to take similar action. This thoughtful and progressive resource management trend will enable park managers to achieve a better balance between the sometimes mutually exclusive National Park Service mission of preserving park resources while providing for their use and enjoyment by people.

A similar trend can be noted in the realm of resource management. For many years, park managers made decisions about resources without the benefit of sound scientific research. Decisions were often made spontaneously—sometimes intuitively—without thorough planning. Today staff scientists advise managers, and fully funded scientific research is conducted on an ongoing basis.

ABOVE: Hale Tharp's log home at the edge of Log Meadow. PHOTO ©RANDI HIRSCHMANN

THE FOOTHILLS

Pictographs near Hospital Rock.　　　PHOTO ©LONDIE G. PADELSKY

My odyssey to the high country begins on the edge of the Central Valley, where a fuzzy, brownish haze forms an artificial western horizon. The pall thins as I travel, but it still carries pollutants that sunlight may transform into ground-level ozone, an invisible gas that is injurious to people and to ponderosa and Jeffrey pines in the forest above. I have chosen to enter the parks through the Ash Mountain gateway. There are no giants here, no spectacle, only the promise of greater things to come. I'm enveloped by uncomfortably warm air, but I catch glimpses of Moro Rock, Castle Rocks, Alta Peak, Mount Silliman, and other lofty sentinels that jut into the cool, clear sky above. They beckon me to climb higher.

Here, the land slopes up from the valley into rolling hills that are brown and sere in summer. But, in early spring, the foothills are green and highlighted with colorful blossoms of California buckeye, redbud, yucca, and a variety of wildfowers. As the summer solstice approaches, the sun begins to bake the hillsides to a golden brown hue that doesn't fade until the return of fall rain. Green ribbons of water-loving alders, sycamores, and willows persist all year along streams that rise in perennial snowfields far above. Really, there are only two seasons here—wet and dry. But, unlike many other places, where summer is a moist and verdant time, in the Sierra many plants wither and die and others become dormant and stop growing until the hottest months are over.

Lowland plants require less water and different soil conditions from those higher up, and the trees are scattered and of small size. The foothills are mostly covered with stunted oaks and grass—a plant community dubbed *chaparral* (meaning "evergreen oak thicket"). *Chaparral* commonly includes dense, wiry carpets of evergreen shrubs called *chamise*. *Chamise* is a member of the rose family with needlelike, olive-green leaves and clusters of small white flowers.

I know that lots of animals live here—critters I might expect to find in a sagebrush *steppe*, or high desert—but I don't see many. Tarantulas, fence lizards, ringtails, loggerhead shrikes, and others are comfortable in the dry heat, yet they live within sight of a forested plateau, where 10 feet of winter snow may accumulate

and temperatures may be 20 degrees or more lower even in summer. Other animals common to the foothills include coyotes, raccoons, striped skunks, acorn woodpeckers, scrub jays, western rattlesnakes, slender salamanders, and pacific tree frogs.

Rising through the foothills I sense subtle variations in temperature and humidity. It becomes cooler and less arid. The character of vegetation and animal life gradually changes, and I recall that climbing higher is like moving farther north. Like their nursery counterparts, wild trees and other plants thrive only when exposure, temperature, water, and soil conditions are right. And, while some animals—mule deer, for example—move freely through different life zones, as people do, many tend to be most comfortable in specific plant communities. That explains why I observe trees, plants, and animals here that I don't see on higher slopes. Organisms at higher elevations are better adapted to colder, wetter conditions.

Sometimes there are variants of similar animals living at different altitudes. For example, the California ground squirrel is at home here in the foothills while its relative, the golden-mantled ground squirrel, frequents the cooler forest. The snowshoe hare dwells in the forest while the related black-tail jackrabbit hops about in the thickets near me.

Living things have adapted to life in the hotter foothills in a number of ways. Plants grow relatively low to the ground, but often have large water and nutrient storing roots. Some have small, thickened leaves that minimize water loss through transpiration. Others enter a state of dormancy to survive the long dry season. Most animals escape the heat by being active nocturnally or at twilight; others seek refuge underground or in the shade of thickets; and, some even produce water metabolically and seldom drink.

At first, the foothills seem ordinary and unimpressive, but they are a biologically rich and diverse part of the greater ecosystem. Still, the subtlety of the foothills may be their salvation. They lack the charisma of the mountains and Big Trees, so they suffer little human impact. It is sometimes very hot and dry here, but the

---

OPPOSITE: Oak woodland in the foothills near the Ash Mountain entrance. PHOTO ©FRED HIRSCHMANN

Lichen-covered granite boulders in oak woodlands near Ash Mountain entrance.

abundant food and cover and the fairly mild year-round climate make the foothills, at once, a harsh but hospitable home for its denizens.

The Generals Highway leads me gradually upward along the lower course of the Kaweah River, below the confluence of its Marble and Middle Forks. Then, near Hospital Rock, an old winter encampment site of the Western Mono people at just under 3,000 feet elevation, the road departs the watercourse and abruptly climbs 12 miles to over 6,000 feet. As I move higher things seem to get bigger, taller, and older.

For me, it's convenient to consider the gross anatomy of the parks as a series of living steps on a geological ladder, but that may belie the unseen connections of the rungs. The foothills, forest, and high country are distinct layers of life, but their edges are not hard and fast. Animals and plants neither see, nor respect, arbitrary boundaries, but the gossamer threads of natural processes such as photosynthesis, the hydrologic cycle, symbiosis, and others bind the life zones and lifeforms into a larger whole.

Redbud and whitethorn in spring bloom.

Seen from the east side of the Sierra Nevada, Mount Whitney rises nearly 10,000 feet above the Alabama Hills.

PHOTO ©LARRY CARVER

In 1889 biologist C. Hart Merriam developed the concept of life zones, belts of vegetation and animal life that are similarly expressed with increases in altitude and latitude. Merriam knew that weather and climate change as one moves from sea level to the summit of a mountain. He suggested that an increase of 1,000 feet in elevation was roughly equivalent to five degrees of latitude—a measure of a location's distance north or south of the equator. Thus, climbing 6,000 feet would be like traveling 1,800 miles north.

Because the sun is directly overhead only at the equator, latitude also indicates the sun's angle of inclination to the earth, and the daily duration and extent of solar heating. In effect the days are longer and hotter at the equator. Since air, land, and water are heated mainly by the sun, Merriam also knew that latitude has a major affect on weather and climate.

Differences in temperature and precipitation that accompany changes in altitude and latitude can cause changes in vegetation and the animal life associated with plant communities. But scientists now know that there are many other factors—soil conditions, water chemistry, slope, exposure, air quality, and others—affecting the vertical distribution of life. While Merriam's Life Zone concept began to shed light on why plant and animal populations differ from place to place in the same region, science has largely discarded it as an over–simplified explanation.

Still, the elevation of Sequoia and Kings Canyon ranges between 1,370 feet, near Ash Mountain, to 14,495 feet, at the summit of Mount Whitney, an elevational difference that creates microclimates from arid desert heat to arctic cold. These chang-

ing conditions favor the development of differing plant communities, with unique habitats and ecological niches, although community boundaries are not fixed.

Generally speaking, there are five fairly distinct vegetation zones on the western slopes of the Sierra. The lower foothills support mostly deciduous trees, such as scrub oak, as well as the evergreen interior live oak, various grasses, and chamise. Manzanita, ceonothus, black oak, incense cedar, and ponderosa pine occur in the upper foothills. The plateau forest is home to white fir, Jeffrey pine, giant sequoia, and a host of understory plants. Lodgepole pine, western white pine, mountain hemlock (very rare), Sierra juniper, and foxtail pine are among the trees of the subalpine forest. Mosses, lichens, and low-flowering alpine plants prevail above timberline.

Formations in Boyden Caverns, Sequoia National Forest.

THE UNDERWORLD

Rock seems to be solid and impervious, yet if you have seen water seep from a spring in a road cut or hillside, you know that some rocks are porous. All surface water doesn't run off into streams and rivers. Sometimes gravity pulls water down into rocks—most often sedimentary ones.

Limestone is especially susceptible to a simple process called carbonation weathering that occurs when particles of rock are dissolved through contact with mild acids. For example, when surface water mixes with carbon dioxide in the atmosphere or the soil, it forms a weak solvent called carbonic acid. This acidic solution seeps into the ground, dissolves the main component of limestone, calcium carbonate, and carries it away, leaving behind caves. While there is little limestone in Sequoia and Kings Canyon, its metamorphic descendant, marble, is common in some areas.

More than 200 caves—some of them quite large—have been discovered in this part of the Sierra. They are formed in marble, which can also be dissolved by acidic groundwater, and contain the full range of features—stalactites, stalagmites, flowstone, and others—found in limestone caves.

Lilburn Cave is the longest cave in California, with nearly 17 miles of surveyed passage. It is etched into beautiful blue-and-white-banded marble, with displays of colorful minerals, including green malachite and blue azurite. Liliburn Cave is not generally accessible, and neither are others like Hurricane Crawl, Soldiers, and Clough Caves.

Crystal Cave is lighted and accessible to visitors. It has been explored by perhaps one million people since it first opened to the public in 1941. It has beautifully banded marble, many cave formations, large rooms, and a spider-web gate made of iron.

Several animals thrive in the sunless subterranean world. Some of them—mostly invertebrates—pass their entire lives in caves; others venture outside from time to time. Many are specially adapted to life underground. Among the full- and part-time residents are bioluminescent millipedes, eyeless centipedes, various spiders, salamanders, bats, an occasional bear, and people. Clough Cave is home to the greatest diversity of animals, including seven species of invertebrates that are possibly found nowhere else in the world.

OPPOSITE: Ornate formation known as "The Dome", Crystal Cave. PHOTO ©LARRY ULRICH

THE FOREST

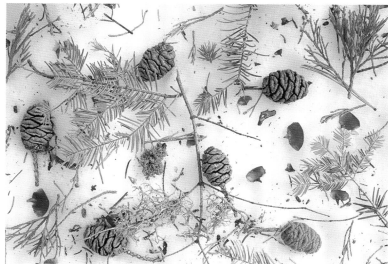

Winter still-life with sequoia cones.

PHOTO©FRED HIRSCHMANN

There are hundreds, perhaps thousands, of other people here, but this Brobdingnagian world is a place for introspection. I need to be alone for a while, save for the company of wild things. Here I renew my connections with nature, and stoke a sense of wonder that sometimes dwindles in my fabricated day-to-day world. Perhaps John Muir stood on this very spot. Surely he felt a great sense of communion with wild things, as I do now.

How can these trees be dated? They seem timeless in human terms. Some began to grow when King Solomon died. Their seedlings breached the soil when Homer wrote *The Odyssey*. Some sequoias were a thousand years old when Christ was born, and when ancient Pinto Indians were building primitive shelters of wood, reeds, and loam in these mountains.

A dozen or so events of world significance mark the passage of my life, but I am an infant among these ancients. The memory of a sequoia tree records hundreds of those happenings. Sequoias are like watchtowers of human history. Cultures have appeared and disappeared. Famous and infamous people have come and gone. Philosophies, religions, and beliefs have evolved. Empires have risen and fallen. Great works of art and industry have been created. Wars have been fought, won and lost. Scientific discoveries and technical advances have been made. All of these things and more have taken place during the life of a single tree that may yet live another thousand years.

I have become trivial among these colossal trees yet, in a cosmic sense, the earth is just a fleck of stardust, and after all, sequoias distill to roots, trunk, and crown. Only the scale is different. Like all living things giant trees need food and water. They breathe, metabolize, reproduce, grow old, and die. Yet, among trees, at least one species lives longer than the sequoia, one is bigger around, and three are taller.

While the General Sherman Tree is the largest living tree, and very old, it is not the oldest. A bristlecone pine—tiny by sequoia standards—holds the record. The oldest tree is rooted in the spare alpine soil of the White Mountains, a range less than a hundred miles east of here. Methuselah, as the tree is known, is believed to be almost 5,000 years old.

Unlike the lofty sequoia, the bristlecone pine is gnarled and twisted by the chilled wind perpetually sweeping through the sparse elfin forest near timberline. The foxtail pine, a relative of the bristlecone pine—and almost as long-lived—is found in the high country of Sequoia and Kings Canyon. These trees are evidence that in nature biggest does not always mean oldest.

Still, a typical mature sequoia's credentials are impressive: 2,000 to 3,000 years old; up to 320 feet tall—taller than the Statue of Liberty; a weight of more than 1,000 tons—as much as eight adult blue whales; largest branch, 4 to 7 feet in diameter—the size of an average tree. A single sequoia tree may produce as many as 2,000 egg-sized cones per year, each containing 100 to 300 seeds. Curiously the seeds weigh only fractions of an ounce, so small that in excess of 90,000 seeds would weigh only a pound.

Sequoia cones may stay green and closed for 20 years or so, unless they are opened by the heat of a periodic wildfire, a hungry Douglas squirrel nibbling on cone scales, or the larvae of tiny cone-boring beetles. Fire is mainly responsible for the release and dispersal of seeds onto the forest floor, where it also creates a fertile ash-laden seedbed.

Most trees die from disease, insect infestations, or fire, but the sequoia usually survives these natural cyclic onslaughts. The giant's weakness lies in its elephantlike feet. Many smaller trees are firmly anchored to the ground by deep taproots. Strangely, a sequoia is precariously attached to the forest floor by a system of shallow roots that seldom reach down more than a few feet. Wind, soil loss, and root damage are like David's sling and stone to this Goliath. Wind sometimes causes sequoias to lose their balance and lean to one side. Eventually, shallow roots loosen their grasp on soil saturated by water or worn thin by millions of human feet. The top-heavy giants fall to the forest floor, succumbing to the main cause of death for sequoias.

At first, the giants command my attention, but there are other trees in this lush forest. Its lower and upper boundaries—about 5,000 and 9,000 feet—are defined by weather. Storms bring 40 to 50

Mountain–pride penstemon and fog along the Alta Trail, Giant Forest.

inches of moisture each winter, mostly in the form of heavy snow, which may accumulate to a depth of 10 feet. Diverse communities of evergreens have adapted to the cold, wet conditions in this snow forest.

I find ponderosa pine and incense cedar on lower, warm, sunny slopes. White pine and sugar pine are a bit higher, found where it is wetter and there is more shade. Still higher, red fir and Jeffrey pine are dominant, but they give way to western white pine, lodgepole pine, and scattered juniper in the upper, colder forest zone. At about 9,000 feet, the forest thins to a few scattered foxtail pines that mark timberline—the upper limit of tree growth. Throughout the forest, most of the other conifers are taller and of greater girth than normal, as if to compete with the mighty sequoias scattered among them.

Foxtail pines near tree-line.

Giant sequoias at the edge of Round Meadow, Giant Forest.

PHOTO ©LARRY ULRICH

Having climbed steeply, more than 3,000 feet from the Kaweah River, the Generals Highway levels out a bit and passes through densely marshaled columns of conifers shrouded in early morning fog. Here is the realm of giants—the gathering of monarchs that John Muir christened "The Giant Forest." It is the first encounter with the Big Trees that folks traveling from the Ash Mountain entrance will have. It's easy to feel like Lemuel Gulliver stepping onto the island of Brobdingnag. Lumber from just one of the sequoias would build 40 five-bedroom houses, with wood to spare.

The forest is like a city of trees built on a gentle incline. This sheltered plateau, and others like it, is called a tableland. Tablelands are characteristic features on the west slope of the Sierra. Millions of years of erosion have roughly leveled the ground, creating high, terraced landscapes bordered by deep canyons that funnel cold, downslope air away from temperature-sensitive sequoias.

Here and there along the outer edge of the plateau, big domes of bare, polished granite expose bedrock that peels away in onion-like layers—a process that geologists call exfoliation. Several of these monoliths, including Moro Rock, Hanging Rock, Sunset Rock, and Beetle Rock, flank Giant Forest and are accessible by trails. A bit farther away, and higher, Castle Rocks overlook the forest. Large luxuriant meadows—Round, Circle, Crescent, Log, Huckleberry—are scattered about like greens on a giant golf course.

The best place to begin an exploration of Giant Forest is in the Giant Forest Museum. It is a recently renovated structure that used to be a part of group of concession facilities providing food and lodging for thousands of visitors. Most of those buildings have been removed, a precedent-setting effort to lessen the impact of human activities on the Big Trees and their companions.

Giant Forest is the home of the General Sherman Tree. It is a giant among giants—the largest tree in the world. Some of its neighbors have intriguing names like the President, Chief Sequoyah, Pillars of Hercules, Chimney Tree, and Burnt Twins. Other sequoias are modest and unnamed, but no less impressive. There are other trees here, mainly uncommonly large sugar pines and white firs, scattered among the sequoias. This is a good place to linger for a while, to get to know the giants better.

PAGE 28/29: Western dogwoods and sequoias in Giant Forest, autumn. PHOTO ©LARRY ULRICH

Giant sequoias and white firs in Grant Grove, winter.

PHOTO ©FRED HIRSCHMANN

The Generals Highway passes through Lodgepole on its way to Grant Grove in Kings Canyon National Park. A stop at Lodgepole Visitor Center will help answer any lingering questions about the Giant Forest area. There are also opportunities to explore the upper reaches of the Marble Fork of the Kaweah River, visit Heather and Pear Lakes, or take longer hikes north to Twin Lakes and the Silliman Crest, or south to Bearpaw Meadow and the Great Western Divide.

After leaving Lodgepole, the highway wends across the plateau to Muir Grove and Lost Grove, which straddle the boundary between Kings Canyon National Park and Sequoia National Forest. Along the way, the highway crosses several streams that are part of the Kaweah River watershed and a small divide that directs water from Dorst Creek into the Kaweah River drainage basin.

Redwood Mountain Grove is not far from Grant Grove. It's one of the largest groves and occupies much of Redwood Canyon. A short side road leads to the site of a former blister rust control camp—where I worked a for a couple of summers, a long time ago. The work involved eradicating plants that served as intermediate hosts for a disease affecting white pine trees. The camp has long since been removed. The site now serves as the beginning of 16 miles of trails that wend through the grove.

Grant Grove is just beyond Redwood Mountain and the Big Stump entrance. It is the site of the General Grant Tree, officially designated The Nation's Christmas Tree and a national shrine honoring America's war dead. Grant Grove was originally part of tiny General Grant National Park, established in 1890 but added to Kings Canyon in 1940.

Big Stump Basin is nearby. It's where logging crews of several men worked for many days to fell sequoia trees—one at a time—more than a hundred years ago. A short trail loops among many stumps. They are sad reminders that even giants eventually fall. Big Stump Basin was added to Kings Canyon National Park in 1958.

A few miles north of Grant Grove, in Sequoia National Forest, lies the Converse Basin. It was the world's largest grove of sequoias, until almost all of them were felled between 1890 and 1906. Unfortunately, only the Boole Tree—the world's eighth largest sequoia—and a few others survived. The Muir Snag was more than 3,000 years old when it died. It was named by John Muir, who discovered it.

OPPOSITE: Giant sequoias in Grant Grove. PHOTO ©LONDIE G. PADELSKY

Giant sequoias in The House Group that have been scorched, but not harmed, by small controlled burns.

FRIENDLY FIRE

To more fully appreciate the role of fire as a natural cyclic mechanism, we need a broader perspective than a human one; we need to think in terms of biogeologic time rather than human time. A human lifetime is inconsequentially brief in an evolutionary context.

Fire has been a natural part of the Sierran ecosystem for centuries. Natural wildfires swept through these plant communities at intervals, providing conditions for many plant species to regenerate. Fire thins competing species, recycles nutrients into the soil, releases and scarifies seeds, and opens holes in the forest canopy for sunlight to enter. All of these are critical to forest health and natural cycles of growth and decomposition.

Fire creates edges, and edges are biologically rich and diverse. Oddly, it helps protect a forest by limiting the build-up of fuels that create very hot, fast-moving, and destructive fires. Periodic fires prevent the invasion of grasslands and meadows by trees; they are, therefore, essential in maintaining equilibrium between forest and grassland. Nutrients are rapidly released from plant materials by fire, thereby contributing to regeneration of both trees and understory plants. Fire-dependent trees such as the sequoia and lodgepole pine have cones that require heat from a forest fire to open, ensuring a ready seed source for seedling establishment immediately following a fire.

Wildfire is a part of the evolutionary history of all wildlife in the Sierra Nevada; still, it may have short-term effects. Fire may temporarily displace animal species dependent on late stages of plant succession, such as the pine marten and the wolverine. Insects may suffer substantial short-term losses, although dung beetles and deer flies have survived here for thousands of years. In birds, the greatest mortality may occur among foragers of the tree trunk and canopy, as well as nestlings.

On the positive side, mule deer, black bears, beavers, mountain lions, and coyotes increase in numbers following fires, due to changes in plant succession and an increase in nutritive forage. Cavity-dwelling birds, such as house wrens, mountain bluebirds, American kestrels, violet-green swallows, tree swallows, and northern saw-whet owls, will increase. Many plant reproductive parts are underground and largely unaffected by fire. Periodic fires with light to moderate heat have little adverse effect on physical and chemical properties of soils.

Author Tom Robbins put things in perspective when he said, "Fire is the reuniting of matter with oxygen. If one bears that in mind, every blaze may be seen as a reunion, an occasion of chemical joy."

OPPOSITE: Fire-scarred members of The Senate Group, Congress Trail. PHOTO ©FRED HIRSCHMANN

Haze and foothills seen from Moro Rock, sunset.

SOMETHING IN THE AIR

A headline in my local newspaper proclaims air pollution in certain national parks is as bad as in some big cities. The article cites a report by the National Parks Conservation Association identifying the five most polluted national parks. Sadly, Sequoia and Kings Canyon were among them, ranking fourth.

The report focuses on an ironic role reversal. Ozone, the same gas that shields us from ultraviolet radiation and moderates the earth's temperature, is a harmful pollutant when it forms near ground level. Ground-level ozone forms when hydrocarbon wastes from car exhausts and emissions from power plants and factories react chemically with each other and produce smog, the brownish haze that I noticed when I entered the park. The chemical reaction is triggered by sunlight, so the amount of ozone in the atmosphere is highest on summer afternoons.

Ponderosa and Jeffrey pine trees are very sensitive to ozone and have shown extensive injury to their foliage, lower photosynthetic rates, and diminished annual ring growth. In contrast with pines, mature giant sequoias seem to be relatively resistant to present ozone levels. However, newly emerged sequoia seedlings are known to be more vulnerable to ozone injury.

Nitrogen is also an essential gas for living things. It's found in the earth and in the atmosphere. Small amounts of nitrogen cycle through the atmosphere, oceans, lakes, streams, plants, and animals. Depending on its form and quantity, nitrogen can be a beneficial nutrient or a toxin, dangerous to people and the environment.

Sequoia and Kings Canyon are not far from greater Los Angeles and San Francisco, and very close to agricultural areas in the San Joaquin Valley. Atomized chemicals from industries, power plants, fertilizers, and insecticides drift into the parks on prevailing winds from the coast.

Scientists believe that these chemicals may be responsible for the failure of peregrine falcons to reproduce and that rising levels of ultraviolet radiation may be involved in the decline of mountain yellow-legged frogs. Many other species may be at risk, too. Park visitors are advised daily of air-quality indexes, to avoid breathing problems and eye irritations.

A non-threatening but egregious effect of air pollution is that it causes a sort of sensory deprivation for visitors by obscuring their view. Forty years ago I saw a false sunset when the sun dropped below a shroud of smog.

CANYON COUNTRY

Cattails in freshwater marsh, Zumwalt Meadows.   PHOTO ©FRED HIRSCHMANN

It may seem trite to call water the lifeblood of living things, but it's true. The cells of animals and plants, including humans, are composed of 70 percent water. I don't hear it sloshing around, but the brain that enables me to perceive, think, and write about this place is 95 percent water. Yet, it's not just the living that must have water. It is an essential part of the life cycle of rocks and mountains, too. Water distills from an oceanic heart; clouds are the arteries that carry it to the land; it falls and is returned to the sea through the veins of streams and rivers.

When Ice Age glaciers melted, they left behind a scoured alpine landscape pitted with shallow depressions in polished and striated rock. These basins catch water melting from remnant ice, perpetual snow, and summer rains that fall before reaching the arid Owens Valley. Hundreds of lakes—3,200 or so—dot the high country. Some, such as Precipice, Arrowhead, Big Bird, Moraine, Bench, and Pear, are named, but many are unidentified. Most lakes release water into the streams and rivers that drain the southern Sierra.

Tulainyo Lake near Mount Whitney lies just short of 13,000 feet. It is the highest lake in the United States and part of a chain of alpine lakes that mark the eastern boundary of the parks. Looking at a map I find names such as Rae Lakes, Dusy Lakes, Kearsarge Lakes, Big Five Lakes, Sixty Lake Basin, and Nine Lakes Basin. The plural names hint at how prevalent lakes are in the high country.

The headwaters of four rivers—the San Joaquin (the South Fork), Kings, Kaweah, and Kern—rise in the high country. The final destination of the Kings, Kaweah and Kern Rivers is the enclosed, southern part of the Central Valley, where they never reach the sea. The South Fork of the San Joaquin River drains to the north, where it joins other rivers draining the Sierra Nevada. Eventually the main body of the San Joaquin River empties into San Francisco Bay. These rivers bring the gift of high Sierra water down to thirsty agricultural lands in the valley. They also provide water for recreational and other human activities

When rain or snow falls, mountains and ridges direct it into drainage basins that funnel water into the rivers. So precise is the division of waters that a knife-edge ridge could split a single drop of rain causing its separated parts to go toward different rivers. Runoff is drawn downward by gravity and seeks the low ground. It gathers in rocky channels and forms tiny rivulets. They grow larger, merge into streams, and then coalesce into rivers that carry cold mountain waters to their distant rendezvous. I imagine myself caught in the hydrologic cycle, a molecule of water falling as snow; melting and trickling slowly into a shallow alpine lake; tumbling down over cascades and cataracts; changing directions to all points of the compass; becoming part of a big river; and, finally returning to the warm Pacific Ocean.

Canyons are formed by fast-flowing water and slow-moving ice. Water-borne abrasives began the process, cutting into granite bedrock, forming angular V-shaped canyons. During the Ice Age, frozen rivers of glacial ice moved down the same canyons, widening them into smoother U-shaped valleys. Today, a few glacial remnants remain, clinging persistently to remote *cirques*, or glacial basins, in the high country.

Water and ice have cut many deep incisions into the rocky flesh of the Sierra. If mountains are the topographic zenith of the Sierra, canyons are the nadir. For every river, there's a canyon it is cutting down between the mountains. Some canyons are named after the rivers that created them—Kings and Kern Canyons, for example. Others such as Enchanted Gorge, and Cloud, Deadman, and Lost Canyons, have names that suggest something about their qualities or things that may have happened there. A few, such as Goddard and LeConte Canyons, are named for people who were integral to the history of the parks or the region.

I'm about half way between Grant Grove and Cedar Grove. Just beyond the park boundary to the north, near where the South and Middle Forks of the Kings River join, the river is 7,800 feet below the summit of Spanish Peak—deeper than in Grand Canyon. Far to the south, the sheer walls of Kern Canyon tower 6,000 feet above the Kern River, and many other canyons exceed 4,000 feet. Near Zumwalt Meadow, I stand at the river's edge and look

---

Mount Mendel, Mount Darwin, and The Hermit rise above McClure Meadow near the headwaters of the San Joaquin River.

up—something that I do frequently in these parks—almost a mile to the top of the canyon walls.

The dimensions of canyons are impressive. Canyons are like mountains in reverse. They simply go down thousands of feet rather than up. But, like everything else in this realm of giants, perceptions depend on perspective. On a mountainside looking down, a canyon looks extraordinarily deep, but on a riverbank looking up, the canyon just seems to make the mountains higher. Either way, there are canyons here to match the beauty and immensity of the mountains.

It's remarkable to me that canyons like this were carved into solid rock by water, and that its work is unfinished. Still, I reflect that in each tiny raindrop or delicate snowflake there is the promise of a river; and, in every river a latent canyon.

Roaring River Falls in Kings Canyon.

South Fork of the Kings River and North Dome in Kings Canyon.

PHOTO ©LONDIE G. PADELSKY

Wherever there are mountains, there will always be canyons and valleys waiting to be revealed by water and ice. There are more than 864,000 acres of high ground in Sequoia and Kings Canyon National Parks, and rivers and glaciers have inscribed dendritic patterns of canyons and valleys into the landscape.

In the geological course of things, land is uplifted, streams become rivers, rivers cut canyons, and canyons become valleys. Canyons are evidence of a river's youth, its proximity to the headwaters. "You can't step into the same river twice," the Greek philosopher Heraclitus wisely said a couple of thousand years ago. In these parks we can see evidence of that truth. Swift mountain water expends most of its energy entrenching the rock, cutting deep and narrow. Old rivers become fat and move slowly through widened channels.

Fast-moving rivers cut down into rock like knives, forming V-shaped canyons. Slow-moving glaciers follow into the same canyons like rasps, changing them into broader U-shaped valleys. The canyon of the Kings River is a work started by a young energetic river but finished by a sluggish glacier. Take a look and you can see it in the wide valley floor, vertical rather than outward-slanted canyon walls, polished rock often marked with horizontal scratches, and water falling from hanging valleys. It's a masterpiece! Upon seeing it, John Muir wrote that it rivaled Yosemite Valley.

Kings Canyon can be reached on a section of State Highway 189 called Kings Canyon Scenic Byway. The road leaves the park near Grant Village and passes through newly authorized Giant Sequoia National Monument, administered by the USDA Forest Service at Sequoia National Forest.

The road into Kings Canyon penetrates more deeply into the heart of the parks than any other. It passes by Cedar Grove, where large incense cedars thrive and add their distinctive fragrance to the valley air, and ends near Zumwalt Meadow. From there trails provide access to Bench, Charlotte, Rae, and other gorgeous lakes, which lie in the morning shadow of the Sierra Crest. On the valley floor it's possible to catch glimpses of glacially sculpted features such as The Sphinx, Sentinel Dome, and North Dome. There are many other canyons in this part of the Sierra, but none that speak more eloquently of the power of water.

The headwaters of the Kern River, Upper Kern Basin. PHOTO ©LONDIE G. PADELSKY

THE RIVERS

John Muir once said, "There is nothing in Nature more eloquent than a mountain stream." Each watercourse has a life, character, and voice of its own. Near its headwaters an infant stream speaks in soft, rippling whispers, sometimes barely audible. Downstream, it matures into a river and talks in rapid, louder tongues, as if drawing attention to its work. At whatever modulation, flowing water speaks in dialects understood by the land and its wildlife. To them it is a prior right.

In a simplified view, rain, snow and high ground are the elements of the river cycle. Gravity is the force that pulls moisture from the clouds, and drives the inexorable flow of runoff toward the distant valleys below. But for gravity to move water over and through the landscape, there must be a gradient, or high ground—whether a few inches or thousands of feet above the level of the sea—and that is the work of geology.

Sequoia and Kings Canyon National Parks average 10,000 feet in elevation, so there is plenty of and enough rain and snow to fill close to 2,600 miles of streams and rivers. During an average year, 40 to 50 inches of precipitation water the plateau forests, and as much as 250 inches of snowfall can build a snowpack of 10 feet or so. The snowpack serves as a storage reservoir that gradually releases water into many drainage basins during spring and summer.

On average, accumulated snow begins to melt by late March and continues through May and June, adding winter's contribution to the parks' streams and rivers. It's at this time that water levels are highest. Sometimes the ordinarily crystalline water is muddied with suspended soil carried down from higher slopes. By early fall, runoff from melting snow has dwindled to nothing, and stream and river flow ebbs. The rivers, and the larger streams that feed them, flow year–round, but some streams are ephemeral, fed only when there is sufficient runoff to fill their channels.

The four principal rivers of the southern Sierra—the San Joaquin, Kings, Kaweah, and Kern—have etched obvious patterns into the landscape. On a map, they look almost like trees with rivers forming the trunks, larger streams the branches, smaller streams the twigs, and lakes and snowbanks the leaves. When I look at these branching patterns, I'm reminded of a Mexican proverb. "He who cares for the tree must also care for the branches." This thoughtful statement applies not just to water but to nature at large. It should be a principle for the wise management of all natural resources because everything in the natural world is connected. It has special meaning to me because I have devoted my adult life to caring for wildlife and wild places.

OPPOSITE: Middle Fork of the Kaweah River near Buckeye Flat, sunset. PHOTO ©JEFF D. NICHOLAS

THE HIGH COUNTRY

Aspen leaves on forest floor.

The summit of Mount Whitney, the tallest mountain in the lower 48 states, is almost three miles above sea level, yet it doesn't seem much taller than its neighbors. It is just one giant among many. More than seventy of the mountains marshaled around Mount Whitney rise above 11,000 feet, twenty are more than 12,000 feet, and six more than 14,000 feet. These frigid windswept heights—born millions of years ago—are big enough and old enough to make a sequoia seem young and small. They represent nature's achievement of perfection in the art of mountain building.

The high country is a blend of lakes, moist meadows, and scattered patches of trees. But mostly, it is vast areas of glacially polished rock, boulder fields, and talus slopes that reflect the morning and evening sun. This is the source of the alpenglow that John Muir called "the divine light" of the high mountains.

Above 9,000 feet, the land and the life forms are very different. The forest thins, sometimes abruptly, as the living conditions become harsher. Short, stocky trees—mostly foxtail pines—give way upslope and on extremely windy ridges to almost barren fields, scattered boulders, and scree.

Above a critical level, the climate becomes too harsh to permit tree growth; low alpine vegetation grows beyond that level. Timberline is the upper limit of tree growth in mountainous regions. Its location depends mostly on temperature but also on soil, drainage, and other factors. The timberline in the Sierra Nevada varies from about 10,000 to more than 11,000 feet.

The cold, windy, and rocky landscape requires special adaptations by living organisms. Low-growing shrubs, flowers, sedges, and grasses dot the landscape. Multicolored lichens cover rocks like a rough, living veneer. It seems odd that many alpine plants have characteristics similar to those that I observed in the foothills environment, such as succulent leaves and large root masses. The common factor is protection from extreme environmental stress.

Higher up, beyond the tree limit, twisted and deformed, shrub-size trees grow. They are called *krummholz*, a German word that means "crooked wood." It is sparse, woody, matlike, and precariously clings to patches of shallow, rocky soil. The climate is cold, and snow may fall at any time, perpetually blanketing much of the glacially polished landscape. This is the alpine tundra—the world near the top—a windswept, treeless area that extends from timberline to the highest mountaintops.

This is the place where clouds come to die. Absorbed invisibly from the warm ocean and lowlands, water clings to motes of airborne dust, which drift inland on unseen currents. The warm, wet air rises. It then cools and more water condenses onto the tiny particles. Clouds are born. The pillows of water vapor drift inland and become larger as they conform to the rising landscape, where the air is even cooler. Water particles coalesce into drops that become heavier and eventually fall as rain or snow, stealing the clouds' identity before they reach the shadow of the eastern escarpment.

In this high place I witness the power of water to wedge and break rocks. Water from rain and melting snow often seeps down into cracks in rocks and cliffsides in the alpine environment. Dramatic variations in temperature cause alternating freeze-thaw cycles. As water freezes, it expands, and if confined in rock fissures, it can exert pressures of almost 30,000 pounds per square inch.

I hear it before I see it. A pika, adding newly cut grass to its winter food cache, is alarmed by my presence and signals its distress with a high-pitched whistle. Nearby, a yellow-bellied marmot, looking a little like a fat woodchuck, drapes itself over a sun-warmed boulder. These high-country dwellers are among the few animals that thrive in this severe environment. Their food is naturally refrigerated. Warm air rising from below carries many insects into the alpine environment, where they die and are frozen into snowbanks, to become food in the spring for American pipits.

Lush meadows of grasses and sedges develop on gentle alpine slopes. They are bright islands of life and color in an otherwise barren environment. Colorful wildflowers, small forbs, shrubs, and cushion plants dot meadows. Patches of lichens brighten drab rock surfaces. Snakelike coils of dirt mark the ground, tracing the underground movements of a pocket gopher.

Trail Crest, south of the summit of Mount Whitney.

I walk across a snowbank and notice that my footprints are the color of watermelon pulp. There's even a faint odor of watermelon. Alpine snowbanks are often colored beautiful shades of red by myriad algal cells—more than a million in a teaspoon of melted snow. During summer, "blooms" of snow algae are often "grazed" by many species of tiny invertebrates, such as snow worms and springtails. Mites, spiders, and insects eat the minute herbivores. They, in turn, are "harvested" from the snow by rosy finches.

Only from this high vantage point can I begin to comprehend the magnitude of this 400,000-acre wild fastness. The sky is crowded with mountains—hundreds, perhaps thousands of shining, silvery-gray peaks and ridges, polished by ice and dappled with snow. They appear to be floating on a darkish, green sea of trees. There are few people here, near the roof of the Sierra. Many of the peaks are humanly accessible with enough time and effort. Today, though, except for a golden eagle soaring past at eye level, I am alone and feel a great sense of tranquility.

The Upper Kern River Basin.

Mosquito Creek, Mosquito Lakes Basin, Mineral King area.

PHOTO ©CARR CLIFTON

Getting high—in the natural sense— is the only way to fully experience the essence of Sequoia and Kings Canyon. While much of the high country can be reached on foot or horseback, many folks can't take the time and effort required to get there. Yet, there is a portal to the high world open to most people. It's a place where you can get to the threshold of the isolated backcountry and begin to sense what the alpine environment is like. It's called Mineral King: a high, undeveloped glacial valley first reached by prospectors searching for silver in 1873.

In 1879, a mining company constructed a narrow, serpentine road that provided access to the valley. Miners did discover some silver, but their dreams of a big strike didn't materialize. Although the mines failed to produce, the road attracted

people interested in other things—logging and possible hydroelectric power development. Still others came to build summer cabins and to ski.

For many years the Mineral King area was part of Sequoia National Forest, where multiple uses were allowed. During the 1960s, proposals to develop a major ski resort resulted in a protracted controversy. Conservationists rallied in defense of this unique vignette of the wild Sierra, squaring off with advocates of development. Congress intervened in 1978 by enacting legislation adding more than 16,000 acres—including the valley, lakes, and surrounding peaks—to Sequoia National Park.

The 25-mile-long road to Mineral King is precipitous. You must carefully negotiate 698 curves— a task that will take at least two hours—but the effort is well worth it. You'll be retracing the steps of

early miners but prospecting for something different: a mother lode of beauty. Here are precious gems! You will strike it rich with splendid views of the prodigious, crenellated Great Western Divide, with nearby Sawtooth Peak and its neighbors all rising above 12,000 feet. Solitude will descend on you in a remote glacial valley perched 7,500 feet above the sea and encircled by granite-capped mountains. Eagle and Mosquito Lakes and other tarns, filling shallow, glacially molded basins, will rival the clarity of any lake you have seen. You can walk among giants in Atwell Grove, higher than any other sequoias. And, you may touch the past at Atwell Mill, where loggers cut nearby timber more than a hundred years ago, or at the ramshackle cabin of James Crabtree, who staked a claim at the White Chief Mine in 1873.

Giant Forest Museum.

MANAGEMENT MILESTONES

The 20-year-long battle to save Mineral King from commercial development as a ski resort ended when Congress rescued the area by adding it to Sequoia National Park in 1978. Speaking for the people, Congress reaffirmed that national parks are the public's domain, not that of special-interest groups. That event was a landmark in conservation history. There have been other victories, other milestones in the management of the precious resources in Sequoia and Kings Canyon, which have required bold action.

Congress established Sequoia and Kings Canyon National Parks—and all other national parks— for the preservation of their resources, and for their use and enjoyment by the people. Preserve and use ...there's the rub. That mandate is a conundrum of sorts, and the National Park Service has had to walk a fine line in its effort to wisely manage the parks while maintaining balance between preservation and use. Still, preservation is the priority, and in recent years park managers have validated that through their actions.

For many years—long before I lived and worked among the Big Trees forty odd years ago—visitor facilities, such as food and lodging,

gas stations, grocery stores, and souvenir shops, were considered essential to visitors' use and enjoyment of Giant Forest, Yet in providing for those concessionaire-operated facilities in a fragile environment, park managers risked compromising the integrity of that environment.

Inevitably, commercial development and years of concentrated human use in Giant Forest began to take their toll on the resources that the National Park Service was charged with protecting. A decision needed to be made, balancing the environmental welfare of the Sequoias with the needs of people.

In 1980, the National Park Service—like Dr. Seuss's Lorax—spoke for the trees. Park managers committed to the removal of most visitor facilities in Giant Forest. It took 15 more years to begin to implement the process, but by fall of 1999, more than 280 buildings—including the one that I had lived in—had been removed, and resources managers had begun restoration projects. In making that bold decision and steadfastly staying on course, the National Park Service not only insured the continued vigor of the forest of giants but also set a precedent for the solution of similar problems in other national parks. By deciding that less is more in this situation, park managers were able to restore the nearly century-long balance between protection and use that is enshrined in the 1916 mission of the National Park Service.

OPPOSITE: Snow covered white firs frame a sequoia trunk in Giant Forest. PHOTO ©JEFF GNASS

THE WILD THINGS

Douglas squirrel, also known as a chickaree.   PHOTO ©CAROL POLICH

It is extraordinarily beautiful in the Sierra Nevada, mountains John Muir called "the range of light." Yet, alone, they are merely cold and inanimate stone—the masonry of geological process. The house that geology built is heated by the fire of the sun, air-conditioned by the wind, and watered by rain and snow. But, it is animated by a fifth essence—myriad plants and animals, which add color, motion, and substance to the barren earth. First, there were empty niches everywhere, but now they are filled. The rock is cloaked in a patchwork of plant and animal communities, even where conditions are extreme, and communities merged to form larger living collectives called ecosystems.

To better understand the wildlife of Sequoia and Kings Canyon I revisit some of the biological concepts I learned long ago. Organisms of the same species have similar characteristics and produce fertile offspring. The place in an ecosystem where a species lives is called its habitat. The function or position of a species in a community is called its ecological niche.

Species are either generalists or specialists. The chickaree is a specialist that feeds mainly on the fleshy scales of conifer trees, including green sequoia cones. The black bear is a generalist that ranges through different life zones eating insects, nuts, berries, and other animals. The beaver—although introduced into the Sierra—is called a keystone species because the ponds it creates by damming provide homes, food, and water for many other living things.

All this organization can be confusing, so I think of it metaphorically. An ecosystem is like a large business or factory. Communities in the ecosystem are like different departments or divisions. Habitats resemble offices or work–spaces. Ecological niches are jobs or occupations. Species are the workers, and some of the workers are specialists, and others are generalists.

All living things are either eating or being eaten. Plants and animals are connected by natural processes such as food chains and predator-prey relationships. These are the ways that energy is moved through an ecosystem. Some living things—plants, for example—are producers; others are consumers; still others are decomposers that recycle nutrients and nurture new life. Simply stated, big fish eat little fish, which eat smaller fish. These relationships form what ecologists call pyramids of numbers and size. Always there are more and smaller individuals at the bottom than at the top, but the amount of energy is constant.

Near the Redwood Mountain grove of Big Trees, I spot a large black bear ambling among the trees and nosing about for gooseberries. It's as if he's here to remind me that in his 200 pounds of bone, muscle, and tendon is concentrated the energy of millions of roots, pine nuts, and berries; thousands of ants, grubs, beetles, and bees; and hundreds of pocket gophers, voles, and fish.

Two and a half centuries ago—about the time that many living Sequoia trees began to grow—Greek philosopher Heraclitus observed that on a circle an endpoint can also be a beginning. And so it goes in nature's house. Grass becomes flesh; flesh becomes grass. A desert cottontail eats grass and is eaten by a bobcat. When the bobcat dies, its remains decompose, returning nutrients to the soil, where they foster the growth of more grass.

In places like this, I witness the intricate workings of natural processes and see that all creatures fill special niches and play important roles in an unending ecological drama. Each species interacts with, and is dependent in some measure upon, the other. Diatoms and rotifers are as important in nature's scheme as a bear. Lichen bearding smaller trees is no less significant than an ancient giant. Ecosystems can be as small as a drop of water, a handful of soil, a vernal pool, or as large as an entire mountain range.

In the foothills, I experience the need for water and shelter from the sun, and I need no explanation why the kangaroo rat and the coyote must cope with dryness and heat. I stand at the edge of a luxuriant meadow stippled with fragrant and colorful spring wildflowers, yet I know that the meadow is an ephemeral garden. I visit a grove of millennia-old, fire-scarred giant trees and learn that they depend on fire for their survival. Scores of birds and small mammals lend motion to the forest as they flit about. At timberline a solitary foxtail pine—more twisted trunk than crown—stubbornly clings to the shallow, rocky soil. In the harsh, inhospitable world near the summit of Mount Whitney, I marvel at the tenacity

Foxtail pine in the austere environment near Tawny Point.

of life in the alpine tundra. Lichens cover rocks like rough, weathered skin, and low-growing plants such as spreading phlox and pussytoes eke out an existence in a place where few animals but birds and bighorn sheep survive. This is what primitive wild America was like.

Yet, I'm sadly reminded of what we have lost in our progress from wilderness pioneers to citizens of a burgeoning technological society. As available living space has dwindled, islands of wilderness like Sequoia and Kings Canyon have become the last refuges for many wild plants and animals. Still, I fear that the security of this place and these living things is an illusion. Harmful winds blow from below, and the ominous dark shadow of the synthetic world looms closer. I pray that it will not write the epitaph for this vestige of the real world.

Mount Russell seen from the summit of Mount Whitney.

OPPOSITE: Lupine and ponderosa pine in Kings Canyon.

Bobcat.   PHOTO ©TOM and PAT LEESON

Yellow-bellied marmot.   PHOTO ©TOM and PAT LEESON

Mountain lion.   PHOTO ©FRANK S. BALTHIS

The term "national park" conjures images of wild animals, large and showy, small and retiring. Sequoia and Kings Canyon are like a giant zoological park covering more than 860,000 acres of diverse wild habitat with no fences, moats, or concrete dens.

The rich and diverse fauna of Sequoia and Kings Canyon is largely distributed along a climatic gradient that ranges from conditions of dry desert heat to moist alpine cold. Animals are specially adapted to the conditions at various elevations, but some are not confined by weather boundaries.

Various insects, lizards, snakes, small rodents, and birds live from about 1,000 feet to 5,000 feet elevation. Expect to encounter scorpions, Boisduval's blue, rosy under-wings, sagebrush lizards, common king snakes, scrub jays, acorn woodpeckers, red-tailed hawks, California ground squirrels, gray foxes, coyotes, bobcats, ringtails, and raccoons. Mule deer are common, but range freely to higher elevations.

A variety of mice, voles, gophers, and ground squirrels live on the forest floor, at elevations between 5,000 and 9,000 feet. Pine martens, porcupines, chickarees, and some-times black bears, are more arboreal. Other residents include montane shrews, mountain beavers, lodgepole chipmunks, montane voles, and snowshoe hares. Steller's jays, Townsend's solitaires, solitary vireos, red-breasted nuthatches, red crossbills, northern goshawks, blue grouse, and great horned owls are common forest birds.

Above 9,000 feet elevation, lies the harsh highcountry. Endangered mountain yellow-legged frogs frequent ponds and lakes. Pikas and marmots search for limited food among the rocks. Bighorn sheep leap easily from rock to rock and climb seemingly sheer cliffs. Clark's nutcrackers busily harvest and cache thousands of conifer seeds, which may be uncovered later by a hungry visiting bear.

White-crowned sparrows, American pipits, rough-legged hawks, and golden eagles are comfortable in the chilly heights. Even the elu-sive wolverine is sometimes seen in the high country.

Canyon country adds other gradients to the animal distribution equation. Since can-yons mark the passage of water from the high country, their floors change elevation depend-ing on the direction of travel. Vertical canyon walls create differing microclimates, too. Many animals characteristic of the different zones through which water flows come to riv-ers to eat and drink. Dippers, harlequin ducks, and great blue herons haunt the riverside, while peregrine falcons and cliff swallows swoop down from canyon walls.

A patient observer can tally more animal sightings than in any zoo, and observe how critters interact in the real world of mountains, forests, and canyons, where nature is the keeper.

Mule deer buck.   PHOTO ©TOM and PAT LEESON

Gray fox.   PHOTO ©TOM and PAT LEESON

Stellers jay.   PHOTO ©FRED HIRSCHMANN

OPPOSITE: Raccoon. PHOTO ©FRANK S. BALTHIS

Rosy fairy lantern.   PHOTO ©LARRY ULRICH

Blazing star.   PHOTO ©CAROL POLICH

Ithuriel's spear.   PHOTO ©LARRY ULRICH

Plants perform many essential functions in these mountains. Green plants are the lungs of the Sierra. Energized by the sun, they combine carbon dioxide with water to produce the oxygen that animals need to breathe and which is an important part of natural processes such as fire, carbonation weathering, and ozone production.

Plants also serve as nature's produce section. When they make oxygen, simple sugars are produced and stored in plant tissues that are eaten by herbivores—nature's vegetarians—such as rabbits, deer, beavers, and squirrels.

Plants are nature's make-up artists, adding a background of green and changing highlights of vibrant color to the drab granite canvas. Many animals are shielded from predators and inclement weather by plants; others use plants as homes and nesting sites. Like animals, plants require certain conditions of temperature and moisture to thrive.

They also need soil that is conducive to growth. Some plants, such as the chaparral yucca, which is pollinated by a single species of moth, require certain animals to ensure their survival.

Wide variations in topography and elevation have created a rich tapestry of plant communities in Sequoia and Kings Canyon. Species range from lichens, liverworts, and ferns to the giant trees, and even include a very small insectivorous plant called the sundew. More than 1,200 kinds of vascular plants have been identified. They follow insects and other invertebrates as the greatest species diversity in the parks.

A kaleidoscopic array of wildflowers bloom in the foothills before the dry season begins. They turn the sere foothills into patchworks of color during the short wet season, then quickly disappear. Flowers to look for between 1,200 and 5,000 feet elevation include Chinese houses, bush monkeyflower, rosy

fairy lantern, baby blue eyes, spice bush, fiesta flower, common madia, wind poppy, Ithuriel's spear, Indian paintbrush, harlequin lupine, and California poppy. California redbud and chaparral yucca also contribute to the show.

From 5,000 to 9,000 feet elevation in the mixed conifer and subalpine forests, expect to see buttercups, American vetch, larkspur, fleabane daisy, columbine, explorer's gentian, mariposa lily, and scarlet gilia. Only a few plants grow in the harsh environment above 9,000 feet. It's cold and windy, the soil is thin, and there is little or no shade. Still, some plants, such as mountain heather, sky pilots, pussytoes, and shooting stars, can be found in moist meadows or rocky clefts. There is a multitude of plants here. Without them, the Sierra would be a lifeless landscape of cold, gray stone.

Mariposa lilies.   PHOTO ©LONDIE G. PADELSKY

Snow plants.   PHOTO ©CAROL POLICH

Miners lettuce and dudleya.   PHOTO ©FRED HIRSCHMANN

OPPOSITE: Leopard lilies in Redwood Mountain Grove. PHOTO ©FRED HIRSCHMANN

Adult black bear and cub.

A WORD ABOUT BEARS

Who has visited a national park and not expected to see a bear? A bear might have been a better choice than a bison to stand next to the sequoia tree on the National Park Service emblem.

Unfortunately the grizzly bear is gone. It took the one-way trip to extinction when it was overhunted, and its habitat grew smaller. Luckily, black bears still range throughout both Sequoia and Kings Canyon, from the foothills to the high country. Chances are you may even spot one during your visit.

Bears are carnivores—complete with sharp claws and teeth designed to tear flesh—but in practice, they are more omnivorous. They eat almost anything and spend most of their time ambling through the forest and foothills searching for food. They tear apart logs, looking for ants and grubs; dig up fleshy roots in meadows; gorge on wild berries, pine nuts, and acorns; sometimes discover a honey tree; and, occasionally kill a rabbit, fawn, or fish. All this eating helps bears to meet their daily needs and bulk up to tide them over the long winter. Black bears may weigh as much as 400 pounds or so.

Too often, bears raid human food left on a picnic table, or, worse, become habituated to human food. They then become "Bad News Bears." Intelligent and opportunistic, they begin to associate people with food and forage for human food instead of natural fare. They become adept at indelicately extracting cookies, marshmallows, candy bars, and other food from cars, trailers, and tents. When this happens bears and people get too close together, and conflicts can arise. People are sometimes hurt, and property is damaged. Sadly, the bear may have to be euthanized to prevent further encounters.

Black bears spend the winter in dens, under large rocks, or among the roots of a rotted tree. Contrary to popular wisdom, bears don't hibernate. Instead they enter a deep winter sleep from which they occasionally awake to venture outside. Tiny bear cubs are born while their mothers are denning. Nourished by their mother's milk, cubs grow rapidly and weigh about five pounds by the time they leave the den in April. Hungry young cubs know little about natural food sources until their mother teaches them, so they may be the first to become beggars and thieves. You can help save a bear by storing food properly and by never giving a bear scraps.

OPPOSITE: Giant sequoia and western dogwood in Redwood Mountain Grove. PHOTO ©LARRY ULRICH

PAGE 60/61: Florence Peak reflected in a backcountry lake. PHOTO ©LONDIE G. PADELSKY

FOR MORE INFORMATION

NATIONAL PARKS ON THE INTERNET:
www.nps.gov

SEQUOIA & KINGS CANYON NATIONAL PARKS
47050 Generals Highway
Three Rivers, CA 93271–9651
(559) 565–3341
www.nps.gov/seki

SEQUOIA NATURAL HISTORY
ASSOCIATION
HCR 89, Box 10
Three Rivers, CA 93271
(559) 565–3759
www.sequoiahistory.org

SEQUOIA FIELD INSTITUTE
(559) 565–4251
E-mail: a-seqnha@inreach.com
www.sequoiahistory.org

THE SEQUOIA FUND
PO Box 3047
Visalia, CA 93278–3047
(559) 739–1668, (559) 739–1680 (Fax)
E-mail: savethetrees@sequoiafund.org
www.sequoiafund.org

GIANT SEQUOIA NATIONAL
MONUMENT
c/o Sequoia National Forest
(559) 784–1500
(559) 338–2251
www.r5.fs.fed.us/sequoia

ROAD CONDITIONS:
(800) 427–7623 (Caltrans)
(559) 565–3341 (N.P.S.)

WILDERNESS PERMIT
RESERVATIONS
Sequoia & Kings Canyon N.P.
HCR 89, Box 60
Three Rivers, Ca 93271
(559) 565–3708, (559) 565–4239 (Fax)
www.nps.gov/seki/bcinfo.htm (info)

VISITOR CENTERS

FOOTHILLS VISITOR CENTER
(Sequoia)
(559) 565–3135

GIANT FOREST MUSEUM (Sequoia)
(559) 565–4480

GRANT GROVE VISITOR CENTER (Kings Canyon)
(559) 565–4307

LODGEPOLE VISITOR CENTER (Sequoia)
(559) 565–3782

CAMPING INSIDE THE PARKS

Reservations for Lodgepole and Dorst Campgrounds
only, all others first–come, first–served:
(800) 365–2267, (888) 530–9796 (TDD)
(301) 722–1174 (Fax)
www.reservations.nps.gov
Reservations may be made up to 5 months in advance

CAMPING OUTSIDE THE PARKS

NATIONAL FOREST RESERVATIONS:
(877) 444–6777 (Reservations)
(559) 338–2251
www.reserveusa.com

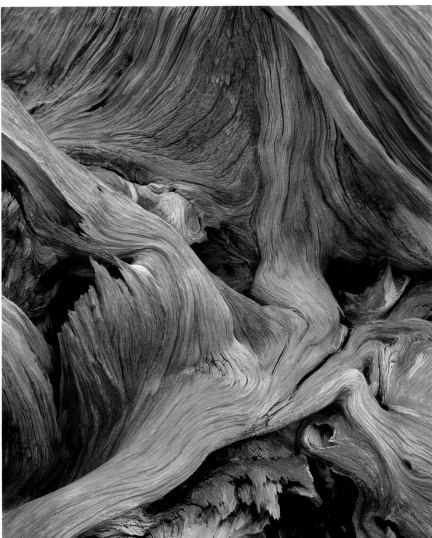

LODGING INSIDE THE PARKS

WUKSACHI VILLAGE (Sequoia)
Delaware North Park Services (DNPS)
Reservations: (888) 252–5757
Front Desk: (559) 565–4070
www.visitsequoia.com

GRANT GROVE LODGE & JOHN MUIR LODGE
Kings Canyon Park Services (KCPS)
(559) 335–5500 (Reservations/Desk)
www.sequoia-kingscanyon.com

CEDAR GROVE LODGE
Kings Canyon Park Services (KCPS)
(559) 335–5500 (Reservations)
(559) 565–0100 (Front Desk)
www.sequoia-kingscanyon.com

SILVER CITY MOUNTAIN RESORT
(Mineral King—Seasonal)
(559) 561-3223 (Summer)
(805) 528–2730
www.silvercityresort.com

BACKCOUNTRY LODGES

BEARPAW MEADOW CAMP (DNPS)
Reservations required: (888) 252–5757
www.visitsequoia.com

PEAR LAKE SKI HUT
Reservations required: (559) 565–3759
www.sequoiahistory.org

LODGING OUTSIDE THE PARKS

MONTECITO-SEQUOIA LODGE
Sequoia National Forest/Monument
(800) 227–9900 (Reservations)
(559) 565–3388 (Front Desk)
www.montecitosequoia.com

STONY CREEK LODGE (KCPS)
(559) 335–5500 (Reservations)
(559) 565–3909 (Front Desk)

KINGS CANYON LODGE
(559) 335–2405 (Reservations)

HISTORIC GUARD STATION (Forest
Service)
(559) 338–3222

THREE RIVERS/LEMON COVE
MERCHANTS
(559) 561–0410, (559) 561–4247 (Fax)
E-mail: merchant@threerivers.com
www.threerivers.com

FRESNO CHAMBER OF COMMERCE
(559) 233–4651

VISALIA CHAMBER OF COMMERCE
(559) 734–5876

SANGER CHAMBER OF COMMERCE
(559) 875–4575

THE RESERVATION CENTRE
(559) 561–0410

CRYSTAL CAVE TOURS

TICKETS MUST BE PURCHASED IN ADVANCE AT
EITHER LODGEPOLE OR FOOTHILLS V.C.

HORSEBACK RIDES

CEDAR GROVE
(559) 565–3464 (Summer), (559) 337–2314 (Off-season)

GRANT GROVE
(559) 335–9292 (Summer)
(559) 337–2314 (Off-season)

MINERAL KING
(559) 561–3039 (Summer)
(928) 855–5885 (Off-season)

ABOVE: Foxtail pine detail. PHOTO ©HOWARD WEAMER

WOLVERTON
(559) 565–3039 (Summer)
(928) 855–5885 (Off-season)

HORSE CORRAL
(559) 565–3404 (Summer)
(559) 564–6429 (Off-season)
(559) 679–3573 (Cell)

OTHER REGIONAL SITES

GIANT SEQUOIA NATIONAL
MONUMENT/SEQUOIA NATIONAL
FOREST
(559) 338–2251

SIERRA NATIONAL FOREST
(559) 855–5360

INYO NATIONAL FOREST
(760) 873–2500

DEATH VALLEY NATIONAL PARK
PO Box 579
Death Valley, Ca 92328
(760) 786–3285
www.nps.gov/deva

MANZANAR NAT'L MONUMENT
PO Box 426
Independence. Ca 93526
(760) 878–2932
www.nps.gov/manz

BOYDEN CAVERN
(Between Grant Grove and Cedar
Grove on Hwy 180
(209) 736–2708

HUME LAKE & BIG MEADOWS
(National Forest/Monument)
Hume Lake District Office
35860 Kings Canyon Road (Hwy 180)
(559) 338–2251

DEVILS POSTPILE NATIONAL
MONUMENT
PO Box 3999
Mammoth Lakes, CA 93546
(760) 934–2289, 872–4881 (Winter)
www.nps.gov/depo

YOSEMITE NATIONAL PARK
PO Box 577
Yosemite National Park, Ca 95389
(209) 372–0200, (209) 372–4726 (TDD)
www.nps.gov/yose

SUGGESTED READING

Arno, Stephen. *Discovering Sierra Trees.* Yosemite and Sequoia National Parks, CA: Yosemite and Sequoia Natural History Associations. 1973.

_____. *Timberline: Mountain and Forest Frontiers.* Seattle, WA: The Mountaineers. 1984.

Basey, Harold. *Discovering Sierra Reptiles and Amphibians.* Yosemite and Sequoia National Parks, CA: Yosemite and Sequoia Natural History Associations. 1976.

Beedy. Edward C/ and Stephen L. Granholm. *Discovering Sierra Birds.* Yosemite and Sequoia National Parks, CA: Yosemite and Sequoia Natural History Associations. 1985.

Despain, Joel. *Crystal Cave, A Guidebook to the Underground World of Sequoia National Park.* Sequoia National Park, CA: Sequoia Natural History Association.

Dilsaver, Larry, and William C. Tweed. *Challenge of the Big Trees: A Resource History of Sequoia and Kings Canyon National Parks.* Sequoia National Park, CA: Sequoia Natural History Association. 1990.

Fowles, John. *The Tree.* W. W. New York, NY: Norton & Company, Inc.. 1983.

Grater, Russell. *Discovering Sierra Mammals.* Yosemite and Sequoia National Parks, CA: Yosemite and Sequoia Natural History Associations. 1978.

Harvey, H. T., H. S. Shellhamer, R. E. Stecker, and R. C. Hartesveldt. *The Giant Sequoia.* Sequoia National Park, CA: Sequoia Natural History Association. 1980.

Hill, Mary. *Geology of the Sierra Nevada.* Berkeley, CA: University of California Press. 1975.

Jones, Charles. *The Gifting Birds: Toward an Art of Having Place and Being Animal.* Salt Lake City, UT: Dream Garden Press. 1985.

National Park Service. *Sequoia and Kings Canyon National Parks Handbook 145.* Washington, DC: Government Printing Office.

Parnall, Peter. *Mountain.* New York, NY: Doubleday. 1971.

Robinson, George B. *Sequoia & Kings Canyon National Parks: In The Company of Giants.* Mariposa, CA: Sierra Press. 1997.

Stone, Christopher D. *Should Trees Have Standing? Toward Legal Rights for Natural Objects.* Los Altos, CA: William Kaufmann, Inc. 1974.

Trefil, James S. *Meditations at 10,000 Feet: A Scientist in the Mountains.* New York, NY: MacMillan Publishing Company. 1986.

Tweed. William C. *A Place for Wonder: The Story of the Giant Forest of Sequoia National Park.* Sequoia National Park, CA. Sequoia Natural History Association. 2002.

_____. *Sequoia & Kings Canyon: The Story Behind the Scenery.* Las Vegas, NV: KC Publications, Inc. 1997.

PRODUCTION CREDITS

Publisher: Jeff D. Nicholas
Author: George B. Robinson
Editor: Nicky Leach
Production Assistant: Melissa Wass
Illustrations: Darlece Cleveland
Printing Coordination: Sung In Printing America

ISBN 1-58071-053-0 (Cloth), 1-58071-052-2 (Paper)
©2003 Panorama International Productions, Inc.

Printed in the Republic of South Korea.
First printing, Spring 2003. Second printing, Summer 2007.

SIERRA PRESS

4988 Gold Leaf Drive, Mariposa, CA 95338
(209) 966-5071, 966-5073 (Fax)
e-mail: siepress@yosemite.net

VISIT OUR WEBSITE AT:
www.NationalParksUSA.com

BELOW
Hamilton Creek and Angels Wings, a location often referred to as Valhalla. PHOTO ©CARR CLIFTON
OPPOSITE
Center Peak and Mount Stanford.
PHOTO ©CARR CLIFTON